BODY IN FLAMES

CUERPO EN LLAMAS

FRANCISCO X. ALARCÓN
TRANSLATED BY FRANCISCO ARAGON

CHRONICLE BOOKS · SAN FRANCISCO

ACKNOWLEDGMENTS
Poems from this collection have previously appeared in the following
publications: *The Berkeley Poetry Review*: "Graffiti," "Grammar,"
"Everything Is an Immense Body," "Body in Flames," "Love Doesn't
Exist," "My Hands"; *City on a Hill*: "So Real"; *Five Fingers Review*: "Old
Song," "Dark Room"; *Lighthouse Point, An anthology of Santa Cruz Writers*:
"A Small but Fateful Victory," "Letter to America"; *Poetry Flash*: "The
Other Day I Ran into García Lorca," "My Bed"; *Practicing Angels, A
Contemporary Anthology of San Francisco Bay Area Poetry*: "Fugitive,"
"Prayer"; *Quarry West*: "Lo del corazón"; *ZYZZYVA*: "I Used to Be Much
Much Darker," "My Hair," "Order in the Home"; *Ya Vas, Carnal*:
"Bridge" (Spanish version only). "Fugitive" also appeared in an
independently produced collection put out by Humanizarte
Publications © 1985; *Tattoos* (© 1985 by Francisco X. Alarcón): "Prayer,"
"Un Beso Is Not a Kiss"; *Lunch Box*: "Punctuation."

Printed in the United States of America.

Library of Congress Cataloging in Publication Data

Alarcón, Francisco X., 1954–
    Body in flames = Cuerpo en llamas / Francisco X. Alarcón ;
translated by Francisco Aragon.
        p.   cm.
    ISBN 0-87701-718-2
    1. Alarcón, Francisco X., 1954–   —Translations, English.
I. Aragon, Francisco.   II. Title.   III. Title: Cuerpo en llamas.
PQ7079.2.A4B6   1990
861—dc20   89-25206
                                                                 CIP

Designed by Karen Pike.

10 9 8 7 6 5 4 3 2 1

Chronicle Books
275 Fifth Street
San Francisco, California 94103

Que no se acabe nunca la madeja
del te quiero me quieres, siempre ardida
con decrépito sol y luna vieja.
          de "El poeta dice la verdad"

Never let it end: this tangle
of I love you you love me, burning
beneath a decrepit sun, an old moon.
          from "The Poet Tells the Truth"

          Federico García Lorca
          Sonetos del amor oscuro (1935)

Contents

3

4

5

Poeta encarcelado

cada mañana
me despierto
solo
fingiendo

que mi brazo
es la carne
de tu cuerpo
sobre mis labios

Imprisoned Poet

every morning
I awaken
alone
pretending

my arm
is your body's
flesh
on my lips

Tan real

todo ha sido
tan real:
las sillas
las puertas
tan sillas
tan puertas

ni un solo día
se ha saltado
el sol:
las noches
han seguido
a los días
y los días
a las noches
tan días
tan noches

todo
tan real y
tan cierto
como mis manos
tus manos
tus labios
y los míos
tan carne
tan sangre

todo
tan realmente cierto
y tan ciertamente real

todo
aún esta voz
que a veces
en el fondo
se sabe
tan incierta
tan irreal

So Real

everything's been
so real:
the chairs
the doors
so chairlike
so doorlike

the sun
hasn't skipped
a single day:
nights
have followed
days and days
have followed
nights
so daylike
so nightlike

everything
so real
so certain
like my hands
your lips
and mine
so fleshlike
so bloodlike

everything
so really certain
and so certainly real

everything
even this voice
that sometimes
deep inside
feels itself
so uncertain
so unreal

I Used to Be Much Much Darker

I used to be
much much darker
dark as la tierra
recién llovida
and dark was all
I ever wanted:
dark tropical
mountains
dark daring
eyes
dark tender lips
and I would sing
dark
dream dark
talk only dark

happiness
was to spend
whole
afternoons
tirado como foca
bajo el sol
"you're already
so dark
muy prieto
too indio!"
some would lash
at my happy
darkness but
I could only
smile back

now I'm not as
dark as I once was
quizás sean
los años
maybe I'm too
far up north

not enough sun
not enough time
but anyway
up here "dark"
is only for
the ashes
the stuff
lonely nights
are made of

En un barrio de Los Angeles

el español
lo aprendí
de mi abuela

mijito
no llores
me decía

en las mañanas
cuando salían
mis padres

a trabajar
en las canerías
de pescado

mi abuela
platicaba
con las sillas

les cantaba
canciones
antiguas

les bailaba
valses en
la cocina

cuando decía
niño barrigón
se reía

con mi abuela
aprendí
a contar nubes

a reconocer
en las macetas
la yerbabuena

In a Neighborhood in Los Angeles

I learned
Spanish
from my grandma

mijito
don't cry
she'd tell me

on the mornings
my parents
would leave

to work
at the fish
canneries

my grandma
would chat
with chairs

sing them
old
songs

dance
waltzes with them
in the kitchen

when she'd say
niño barrigón
she'd laugh

with my grandma
I learned
to count clouds

to point out
in flowerpots
mint leaves

mi abuela
llevaba lunas
en el vestido

la montaña
el desierto
el mar de México

en sus ojos
yo los veía
en sus trenzas

yo los tocaba
con su voz
yo los olía

un día
me dijeron:
se fue muy lejos

pero yo aún
la siento
conmigo

diciéndome
quedito al oído
mijito

my grandma
wore moons
on her dress

Mexico's mountains
deserts
ocean

in her eyes
I'd see them
in her braids

I'd touch them
in her voice
smell them

one day
I was told:
she went far away

but still
I feel her
with me

whispering
in my ear
mijito

First Day of School

frente
a la teacher

apreté
más fuerte

la mano
de mi abuela

la teacher
se sonrió

y dijo algo
raro en inglés

mi abuela
luego me dio

su bendición
y se fue

yo me quedé
hecho silla

en un mundo
muy extraño

First Day of School

standing before
the teacher

I squeezed
my grandma's

hand
harder

the teacher
smiled

and said something
odd in English

then my grandma
gave me

her blessing
and left

I stayed behind:
a chair

in a very strange
world

La Misión

San Francisco

buenos días
colores
vida mía

buenas tardes
risas
pan de olor

cómo están
gente
mitorera

puertas tristes
música
de ventanas

caras jóvenes
riqueza
de los más pobres

un día
yo puedo dejar
el barrio

pero éste
nunca saldrá
de mí

The Mission

San Francisco

good morning
colors
life of mine

good afternoon
laughter
fragrant bread

what's new
people
the latest gossip

sad doors
music
from windows

young faces
riches
of the very poor

one day
I may leave
this place

but el barrio
will never
leave me

Graffiti

por nuestro
pueblo
hablarán
estos muros

elocuentes
apuntarán
así amaron
esos locos

hermosas
sinfonías
saldrán
de garabatos

ahí mismo
quedará
nuestra vida
por descifrarse

Graffiti

on behalf
of our people
these walls
will speak

eloquent
they'll point out:
those locos loved
like *this*

beautiful
symphonies
will emerge
from scrawls

and there also
will remain
our lives
to be deciphered

Lavaplatos

rumbo
a la escuela
de noche

caminaba
sonriendo
por la Misión

bajo
el brazo
moreno

su libro
de aprender
inglés

recién
bañado
vi a Dios

Dishwasher

on his way
to night
school

he walked
smiling
through the Mission

beneath
his brown
arm

his book
for learning
English

freshly
bathed
I saw God

Gramática

en mi mundo
hay poco lugar
para adjetivos

un caldo de res
se coce diario
sobre las estufas

la ropa se seca
en las ventanas

la gente baila
en vez de hablar

en las calles queda
tanto por nombrar

en mi mundo
todos los nombres
se vuelven verbos

y todos los verbos
se conjugan igual
que el verbo "vida"

Grammar

in my world
there's little room
for adjectives

beef stew
is cooked daily
on stoves

clothes are dried
from windows

instead of talking
people dance

so much remains
to name on the streets

in my world
all names
become verbs

and all verbs
conjugate the same
as the verb "life"

Puntuación

mis poemas
no usan
puntos
o comas
sólo
cagaditas
de mosca   .

Punctuation

my poems
don't use
periods
or commas
only tiny
pellets
of fly shit

•

Antigua canción

todos llevamos
en el pecho
una canción

tan antigua
que no sabemos
si la aprendimos

cualquier noche
entre el rumor
de besos caídos

nuestros labios
nos sorprenden
al entonar

esta canción
que es canto y
llanto a la vez

Old Song

each of us carries
in our chest
a song

so old
we don't know
if we learned it

some night
between the murmurs
of fallen kisses

our lips
surprise us
when we utter

this song
that is singing
and crying at once

Consejos de una madre

hijo
ya cruzas
los 33 años

y no veo
asientes
cabeza

mira
tu mundo
alrededor

tus primos
están todos
bien parados

con los pies
plantados
en la tierra

mientras tú
me duele
verte así

gastando
tus ojos
y tu tiempo

en eso
que llamas
poemas

Advice of a Mother

hijo
you've
turned 33

yet I see
you heading
nowhere

look at
the world
around you

your cousins
are all
standing firm

their feet
planted
on the ground

while you
it hurts to
see you this way

wasting
your eyes
and your time

with those things
you call
poems

2

Cuarto oscuro

en cada casa
hay un cuarto
oscuro

enclaustrado
entre paredes
de otro cuartos

a los hombres
no les parece
molestar

lo consideran
lo más normal
de la vida

pero viven ahí
en esa mazmorra
sin ventanas

la madre
la hija
la esposa

Dark Room

in every house
there is a dark
room

hidden
by the walls
of other rooms

it doesn't seem
to bother
men

they consider it
the most normal thing
in life

but there inside
that cell without
windows live

the mother
the daughter
the wife

Mi padre

mi padre
y yo nos
saludamos

cautelosos
como si
selláramos

una tregua
en un campo
de batalla

nos sentamos
a comer como
dos extraños

yo sé que
en el fondo
él también

desecha
ese mal
esa locura

esa pesadilla
llamada
hombre

My Father

my father
and I greet
each other

cautiously
as if
sealing

a truce
on a
battlefield

we sit down
to eat like
two strangers

yet I know
beneath it all
he too

rejects
that affliction
that folly

that nightmare
called
man

Una pequeña gran victoria

esa noche de verano
mi hermana dijo
     no
ya nunca más
se iba a poner ella
a lavar los trastes

mi madre sólo
se le quedó viendo
quizás deseando
haberle dicho
lo mismo
a su propia madre

ella también había odiado
sus tareas de "mujer"
de cocinar limpiar
siempre estar al tanto
de sus seis hermanos
y su padre

un pequeño trueno
sacudió la cocina
cuando silenciosos
nosotros recorrimos
con los ojos la mesa
de cinco hermanos

el repentino aprieto
se deshizo cuando
mi padre se puso
un mandil y abrió
la llave del agua
caliente en el fregadero

A Small but Fateful Victory

that summer night
my sister said
        no
never again
she wasn't doing
the dishes anymore

my mother
could only stare
maybe wishing
she had said
the same thing
to her mother

she too had hated
her "woman" chores
of cooking cleaning
always looking
after six brothers
and her father

a small thunder
shook the kitchen
as we quietly
exchanged looks
around the table
of five brothers

the impasse broke
when my father
put on an apron
and started to run
the hot water
in the sink

yo casi podía oír
la dulce música
de la victoria
       resonando
en los oídos de mi hermana
en la sonrisa de mi madre

I could almost hear
the sweet music
of victory
            ringing
in my sister's ears
in my mother's smile

Prófugo

he tenido
que soportar
los días
anónimo
como sombra
escurrirme
por la ciudad
sin causar
sospecha

he rodeado
innumerables
caminos
saltado
cada cerca
huyendo
siempre
con una prisa
que me muerde
los talones
y apenas
me deja
respirar

ocultándome
tras tantas
quimeras
durante
tantos años
que ahora
ya ni distingo
el rostro de
mi alma
ni recuerdo
qué me llevó
a esta vida
de prófugo

Fugitive

I've had
to bear
the days
anonymously
like a shadow
slip
through the city
without raising
suspicions

I've avoided
countless
roads
jumped
every fence
always
fleeing
with a haste
that bites
my heels
and barely
lets me breathe

hiding behind
so many illusions
for so
many years
that now
I don't
even know
the face of
my soul
nor recall
what brought me
to this fugitive's life

mi crimen
debe haber
sido enorme
como
la oscuridad
que acarrea
mi pena

ante todo
he procurado
la compañía
muda
de la noche

he aprendido
a disimular
casi todo
pero
todavía
me delata
junto a ti
el desbocado
palpitar
de mi corazón

my crime
must have
been
as huge as
the darkness
found in
my punishment

above all
I've sought
the mute
company
of night

I've learned
to fake
nearly everything
but
still
when next to you
I'm given away
by the empty
pounding
of my heart

Naturaleza criminal

soy
un nómada
en un país
de sedentarios

una gota
de aceite
en un vaso
de agua

un nopal
que florece
en donde
no se puede
ni se debe
florecer

soy
una herida
todavía viva
de la historia

mi crimen
ha sido ser
lo que he sido
toda mi vida

Natural Criminal

I am
a nomad
in a country
of settlers

a drop
of oil
in a glass
of water

a cactus
that flowers
where one
can't
and shouldn't
flourish

I am
history's
fresh and
living wound

my crime
has been being
what I've been
all my life

Tropical

allá no hablo
canto
arpa se vuelve
mi corazón

allá no miro
pinto
hojas les salen
a mis manos

allá soy pájaro
pez fruta río
soy sierra verde
estela y sol

aquí sólo soy
una voz
que clama
entre el cemento:

"yo soy un hombre
tropical"

Tropical

down there I don't speak
I sing
my heart growing
strings

down there I don't see
I paint
my hands sprouting
leaves

down there I am a bird
a fish a fruit a river
a green mountain range
carved stone the sun

up here I am just
a voice
that clamors
bounces off concrete:

"I am a tropical
man"

Un Beso Is Not a Kiss

un beso
es una puerta
que se abre
un secreto
compartido
un misterio
con alas

un beso
no admite
testigos
un beso can't
be captured
traded
nor sated

un beso
is not just
a kiss
un beso is
more dangerous
sometimes
even fatal

El otro día me encontré a García Lorca

lo reconocí
por el moño
los labios
los ojos
olivos

lloraban
guitarras
y bailaba
flamenco
la tarde

de pronto
se paró
vino
directo
a mi mesa

y me plantó
un beso
como sol
andaluz
en la boca

The Other Day I Ran into García Lorca

I recognized him
by the slim bow tie
his lips
his eyes
olive-colored

guitars
wept and
the afternoon
danced
flamenco

suddenly
he stood
walked
directly
to my table

and planted
a kiss
like an Andalusian
sun
on my lips

Centroamérica en el corazón

la última
mirada de
los jóvenes
desaparecidos
en plena flor
la llevamos
cosida bajo
los párpados

el grito de
las madres
al reconocer
la camisa
balaceada
nos atraviesa
la sien hasta
los talones

las montañas
verdiazules
los amaneceres
despejados de
Centroamérica
nos reclaman
toda la sangre
derramada

inocente sangre
de monjas
de maestros
de señoras
con mandil
de niños
¡cuál infame
matadero!

ahora ya
no tenemos
escapatoria

Central America in the Heart

the last
expression
of the disappeared
young
in full bloom
we carry
stitched beneath
our eyelids

the wail
of mothers
upon recognizing
the bullet-ridden
shirt
pierces us
from head
to toe

the bluegreen
mountains
the dawns
bright and clear
of Central America
demand back
all spilled
blood

innocent blood
of nuns
of teachers
of women
in aprons
of children
that infamous
slaughterhouse!

and now
we have no
escape

esta guerra
desencarnada
nos ha puesto
¡una bomba
en el corazón!

this war
disembodied
has placed
a bomb
in our heart

Pobres versos

qué ganamos
con escribir
los versos
más tristes
esta noche

usar la tinta
más amarga
hasta hacer
pañuelo
el papel

cuando ellos
se burlan
de nosotros
con sus armas
ensangrentadas

Pathetic Lines

what do we gain
writing
the saddest
lines
tonight

using ink
so bitter
it makes
tissue
out of paper

when they
scoff and
jeer at us
their arms
covered with blood

Las Flores Son Nuestras Armas

we opened
the doors
of our homes

to greet them
they came in
and evicted us

we showed them
the open green
of our valleys

the sacred
blue
of the sky

they cut down
the trees
for their furnaces

we gave them
the fruits
of this land

they poisoned
the rivers
with mercury

yet we survived
the slaughter
of our days

and now we face them
in this final
battle

to save
our lives
the lives of all

desierto/desert
give us
your strength

viento/wind
blow into us
your courage

madre agua
guide us in
your tender ways

carnalitos
y carnalitas
brothers
and sisters
don't be afraid

las flores
las plumas
the flowers
the feathers
are
on our side!

3

Todo es un cuerpo inmenso

todo es
un cuerpo
inmenso

las sierras
muslos
extendidos

los árboles
en el valle
pelo en pecho

las bahías
bocas
lengua el mar

Everything Is an Immense Body

everything is
an immense
body

the sierras
extended
thighs

the trees
in the valley
hair on a chest

the bays
mouths
tongue the sea

Caracol

le digo
chistes
al oído

el mar
se ríe
a olas

Seashell

I tell it
jokes
in its ear

the sea
laughs
waves

Anatomía presagiosa

qué noches
guardan callados
tus brazos

qué auroras
prometen tiernos
tus labios

qué brisas
cargan gustosos
tus hombros

qué tempestades
avecinan
sin saberlo
tus cabellos

qué hogueras
qué precipicios
qué heridas
anuncian
acaso proféticos
tus ojos

Prophetic Anatomy

what sort of nights
do your arms gather
in silence

what sort of dawns
do your lips
tenderly promise

what sort of breezes
do your shoulders carry
without complaint

what sort of storms
does your hair
unknowingly
predict

what sort of fires
what sort of cliffs
what sort of wounds
are announced
by your possibly
prophetic eyes

Puente

extiende
los brazos
extiéndelos
que toquen
tus manos
mi orilla

yo recorreré
tu cuerpo
como quien
cruza
un puente
y se salva

Bridge

extend
your arms
extend them
until your hands
touch the edge
of my body

I will travel
across your body
like someone
who crosses
a bridge
and saves himself

Cuerpo en llamas

quiero dejar
las palabras

ir y despertar
los sentidos

no quiero
la memoria

sino abrazar
cada instante
hasta la locura

quiero pensar
con los pies

quiero llorar
con los hombros

quiero prender
fuego al cuerpo

Body in Flames

I want to abandon
words

go and awaken
the senses

I want no
memory

rather to embrace
every instant
to a frenzy

I want to think
with my feet

I want to cry
with my shoulders

I want to set
my body on fire

El amor no existe

el amor
no existe
me dices

mentira
que haya
amantes

es puro
invento
de tontos

me explicas
ocultando
tu sorpresa

al ver en
el cristal
del café

a nuestras
dos sombras
abrazándose

Love Doesn't Exist

love
doesn't exist
you tell me

it's a lie
that there are
lovers

the pure
invention
of fools

you explain
concealing
your surprise

as you notice
in the window
of the café

both of our
shadows
embracing

Mis manos

yo no tengo
otros ojos
que mis manos

ni más boca
corazón
que mis manos

temblorosas
se acercan
hacia a ti

en lo oscuro
de la noche
te ven te hablan

My Hands

I have no
other eyes
than my hands

nor more of a mouth
a heart
than my hands

trembling
they close in
on you

in the dark of night
they see you
they speak to you

Mi cama

es la balsa
en que navego
todas las noches
buscando salvar
los restos
de mi naufragio

es el muelle
de mi pobre
puerto
que con ansias
espera regresen
los marineros

es mi isla
perdida
mi alberca
mi cuadrilátero
lo que me queda
de árabe

es mi último
refugio
mi nido
mi tumba
el único altar
de mi casa

My Bed

it is the raft
on which I navigate
every night
looking to salvage
the remains
of my shipwreck

it is the dock
in my poor
harbor
that with longing
awaits the return
of sailors

it is my lost
island
my cistern
my boxing ring
the trace of Arab
left in me

it is my last
refuge
my nest
my tomb
the only altar
in my home

Orden en la casa

me reclamas
porque dejo
toallas húmedas
sobre la cama

todas las cosas
tienen su lugar
me aleccionas
recogiendo

los libros
amontonados
en la mesa
de la cocina

yo me apresuro
y cubro con
mi cuerpo
los calzones

que relucen
como sonrisa
sobre el sofá
rojo de la sala

Order in the Home

you complain
because I leave
damp towels
on the bed

all things
have their place
you lecture me
gathering

the pile
of books
off the kitchen
table

I hurry
and cover with
my body
the underwear

that gleams
like a smile
on the red
living room sofa

Lo del Corazón

the heart is
too wrapped up
to account
for love

toes are
the true markers
of warm
loving nights

Mi pelo

cuando
me conociste
mi pelo era
negro como
el más negro
lienzo

con tu pelo
haré finos
pinceles
me decías
mordiéndome
las orejas

y yo corría
con mi pelo
negro suelto
como potro
reluciendo
su negra crin

con tus canas
ahora hice
una larga soga
me dices
amarrándome
el cuello

My Hair

when
you met me
my hair was
black like
the blackest
canvas

with your hair
I'll make the finest
paintbrushes
you·would tell me
biting
my ears

and I would run
with my black
hair loose
like a colt
its black mane
shining

with your gray hair
I've made now
a long rope
you tell me
wrapping it
around my neck

4

Mis muertos

un día lluvioso
me dieron lástima
y los dejé entrar
desde entonces
mis muertos y yo
somos inseparables

me acompañan
a donde yo vaya
unos son alegres
otros pensativos
todos me cuentan
historias increíbles

hay uno simpático
que al hablarme
me agarra las manos
el pobre insiste:
"mírame bien porque
éste que ves eres tú"

My Dead

one rainy day
I felt pity
and let them in
since then
me and my dead
are inseparable

they tag along
wherever I go
some are cheerful
others pensive
all tell me
incredible stories

the good-natured one
when speaking to me
grabs hold of my hands
the poor guy insists:
"take a good long look
this one you see is you"

Funeral

¿a dónde
con tanta
prisa?

¿para qué
tantos
ramilletes?

¿de dónde
tanta
lágrima?

si al fin
y al cabo
nada resiste

la lluvia
la muerte
el tiempo

como el kleenex
tirado junto
al foso

del último
clímax velado
de la viuda

.

Funeral

where to
in such
a hurry?

why
so many
bouquets?

from where
so many
tears?

if in the end
nothing
resists

the rain
death
time

like the kleenex
tossed beside
the grave

of the widow's
last
veiled climax

Asalto

live fast/die young
　　　—Tatuaje

confieso
que me dolió
verme tendido
en un charco
de mis venas
una y otra vez
atravesado
los bolsillos
al revés

me dolía
despedirme
así no más
tan sin aviso
que el aire
de la noche
se hiciera piedra
y un hilo roto
mi memoria

al momento
que entregaba
mi cartera
mi reloj
me dio risa
el filoso brillo
de la navaja
aquel tatuaje
mi vida entera

"man
what's
so funny"
bulbuceó
temeroso
mi asaltante

Assault

live fast/die young
          —Tattoo

I confess
it hurt to see
myself lying
in a puddle
my veins opened
once and again
knifed
my pockets
inside out

it hurt
to say goodbye
just like that
so suddenly
the night
air became
a stone
my memory
a broken string

at the moment
of surrendering
my wallet
my watch
I laughed
at the knife's
sharp brilliance
my whole life
that tattoo

"man
what's
so funny"
stammered
my assailant
nervously

luciendo pecas
y zapatos
de charol

luego
oí unos pasos
que corrían
tras la llovizna
en plena calle
recordé que
ya era sábado:
yo todavía
seguía vivo

flashing his freckles
and varnished
shoes

and then
I heard
in the drizzle
running steps
remembering
as I stood in the street
it was Saturday:
I was still
alive

Las palabras agonizan

las sílabas
lloran
las pobres
ya como
huérfanas

los párrafos
carilargos
¿a quién
le gusta
enviudar?

las palabras
están muy
pero muy
graves en
el hospital

The Words Are Hurting

the syllables
are crying
the poor things
just like
orphans now

the paragraphs
are long-faced
who here wants
to become
a widower?

the words
are in very
but very
critical condition
in the hospital

Oración

quiero un dios
de cómplice
que se trasnoche
en tugurios
de mala fama
y los sábados
se levante tarde

un dios
que chifle
por las calles
y tiemble
ante los labios
de su amor

un dios
que haga cola
a la entrada
de los cines
y tome café
con leche

un dios
que escupa
sangre de
tuberculoso
y no tenga ni
para el camión

un dios
que se desmaye
de un macanazo
de policía
en un mitin
de protesta

un dios
que se orine

Prayer

I want a god
as my accomplice
who spends nights
in houses
of ill repute
and gets up late
on Saturdays

a god
who whistles
through the streets
and trembles
before the lips
of his lover

a god
who waits in line
at the entrance
of movie houses
and likes to drink
cafe au lait

a god
who spits
blood from
tuberculosis
and doesn't even have
enough for the bus

a god
knocked
unconscious
by the billy club
of a policeman
at a demonstration

a god
who pisses

de miedo ante
el resplandor
de los electrodos
de tortura

un dios
que le punce
hasta el último
hueso
y muerda el aire
de dolor

un dios desempleado
un dios en huelga
un dios hambriento
un dios fugitivo
un dios en exilio
un dios encabronado

un dios
que anhele
desde la cárcel
un cambio
en el orden
de las cosas

quiero
un dios
más dios

out of fear
before the flaring
electrodes
of torture

a god
who hurts
to the last
bone
and bites the air
in pain

a jobless god
a striking god
a hungry god
a fugitive god
an exiled god
an enraged god

a god
who longs
from jail
for a change
in the order
of things

I want a
more godlike
god

Epitafio

siempre
preferí
la sombra
de un árbol
a la custodia
de una catedral

Epitaph

I always
preferred
the shade
of a tree
to the custody
of a cathedral

5

Carta a América

perdona
la tardanza
en escribirte

a nosotros
nos dejaron
pocas letras

en tu casa
nos tocó
ser tapetes

a veces
de pared
pero casi

siempre
estuvimos
en el piso

también
te servimos
de mesa

de lámpara
de espejo
de juguete

si algo
te causamos
fue risa

en tu cocina
nos hiciste
otro sartén

todavía
como sombra
nos usas

Letter to America

pardon
the lag
in writing you

we were left
with few
letters

in your home
we were cast
as rugs

sometimes
on walls
though we

were almost
always
on floors

we served
you as
a table

a lamp
a mirror
a toy

if anything
we made
you laugh

in your kitchen
we became
another pan

even now
as a shadow
you use us

nos temes
nos gritas
nos odias

nos tiras
nos lloras
nos niegas

y a pesar
de todo
nosotros

seguimos
siendo
nosotros

América
entiende
de una vez:

somos
las entrañas
de tu cuerpo

en la cara
reflejamos
tu futuro

you fear us
you yell at us
you hate us

you shoot us
you mourn us
you deny us

and despite
everything
we

continue
being
us

America
understand
once and for all:

we are
the insides
of your body

our faces
reflect
your future